CW00405579

Christianity

An Introduction to the Catholic Faith

by
David Albert Jones

*All booklets are published thanks to the
generous support of the members of the
Catholic Truth Society*

CATHOLIC TRUTH SOCIETY

PUBLISHERS TO THE HOLY SEE

Nihil obstat: Robert Ombres, O.P. (Censor)

Imprimatur: Malcolm McMahon, O.P. (Prior Provincial)

All rights reserved. This edition first published 2012 by The Incorporated Catholic Truth Society, 40-46 Harleyford Road London SE11 5AY Tel: 020 7640 0042 Fax: 020 7640 0046. Copyright © 2012 The Incorporated Catholic Truth Society. Scripture quotations are taken from the RSV Catholic Edition.

ISBN 978 1 86082 809 6

For all those who,
holding to the truth,
hand on the catholic and apostolic faith.
(Eucharist Prayer I)

Table of Contents

The Aims of this Booklet

This booklet aims to give a general introduction to the Catholic faith for someone who is open or sympathetic and who wishes to get some overview of the faith as a whole. This means that no teaching is treated with the depth it deserves, but it is hoped that the shape of the whole emerges quite well. It is a sort of map of the Catholic understanding of God and his revelation in Jesus.

This booklet was first published by Family Publications of Oxford, and was commissioned jointly by the Catholic Society, the Catholic Graduate Society and the Newman Society, all of Oxford University. A later edition was produced by the Dominican Friars to coincide with the 2008 World Youth Day in Sydney, Australia.

The present edition has been produced by the Catholic Truth Society for the Year of Faith 2012.

David Albert Jones is director of the Anscombe Bioethics Centre in Oxford, research fellow at Blackfriars Hall, Oxford and visiting professor at St Mary's University College, Twickenham. He read Natural Sciences and Philosophy at Cambridge, and Theology at Oxford. His publications include *The Soul of the Embryo: An enquiry into the status of the human embryo in the Christian tradition* (Continuum, 2004), *Approaching the End: a theological exploration of death and dying* (Oxford University Press, 2007) and *Angels: A Very Short Introduction* (Oxford University Press, 2011). He is married and lives in Oxford.

I. The Mystery of God

God

Every house is built by someone,
but the builder of all things is God. (Hebrews 3:4)

There was a time when you did not exist. Each of us is like a world in itself, a conscious light on the world, and yet we each had a beginning and will have an end. We were brought into existence by others, and are constantly sustained by many causes, inside and outside ourselves. We have a small place in a great universe made of many parts that come to be and pass away, and each depends on others for its beginning and its continued existence. But what about the universe *as a whole*? Is it a necessary thing that exists of itself? How can it be, if it is made up of all these parts, each of which depends on others? There must be something necessary and unchanging that grounds and sustains our changing world.

Some think that this necessary and unchanging thing is a mathematical equation, one that will explain why physical laws are the way they are. But a mathematical equation on its own cannot cause or sustain anything. It is a sort of description, not a real thing. We are left wondering not *how* the world is, but *that* the world is. As the physicist Stephen

Hawking once asked, "What is it that breathes fire into these equations and makes there a world for them to describe?"

This question demands an answer, which cannot be a cause within this universe of causes, which cannot be changeable or complex or made of many parts, which cannot depend on anything outside itself. It points beyond the whole universe to a place where ultimately the buck *stops*. There is some *necessary* being, the cause and sustainer of *all* realities, all life and being, all intelligibility. This is what gives the world its very existence, without which the world would not be there at all. This is the one true God, the creator of all things visible and invisible, who brought all things to be out of nothing, and who holds all things in the palm of his hand (*Rm* 1:19-20; *Ws* 13:1-9).

Some things are easy to understand and others more difficult, but the most profound realities can never be understood completely. Before them we are like bats blinded by the sunlight. Such realities are too great for us to grasp. A truth that the mind can partly understand but never fully comprehend is called a *mystery*. God is the first and greatest mystery. We can know the things that God has made, and perhaps they show us something of their cause (the source of all *being*, all *life*, all *creativity*, all *love* and *knowledge*). Yet for every similarity between creature and creator there is always a greater dissimilarity. We cannot know what God is in God-self. This is what the Holy Scriptures say: "No one can see the face of God and live." (*Ex* 33:20). Even "the appearance of the likeness of the glory of the Lord" (*Ezk* 1:28) was too much for the prophet to behold. God is a great mystery, a fearful and transcendent reality.

To believe in God, then, is not to understand and identify yet one more object in the universe. It is rather to believe that the whole universe has direction and meaning, source and end. The universe may be vast and earth small in comparison, but the size of the scenery is not what gives significance to the play. It is the characters who make the plot, and the life and thought and love that exist on earth are of more significance than giant stars and gas clouds and empty spaces, no matter how immense.

If there is one source of being, then not only great events and general laws but every event within the life of each creature will have its ultimate cause in that source. God is at the centre of everything he has made, holding it continually in being. He is closer to us than we are to ourselves. Jesus Christ said, "Are not two sparrows sold for a penny? And not one of them will fall to the ground without your Father's will. But even the hairs on your head are numbered. Fear not, therefore, you are of more value than many sparrows." (*Mt* 10:29-31). To believe in God is to believe that there is a meaning to the universe as a whole, a meaning that includes all human life and even the day-to-day events of your life (*Ps* 139). It is to believe that there is a guiding hand in history, deeply mysterious but nonetheless able to fulfil the ultimate purpose of our life. This is called the doctrine of Providence.

The People of God

The Lord said to Abram, "Go from your country and your kindred and your father's house to the land that I will show you. And I will make of you a great nation, and I will bless you and make your name great, so that you will be a blessing." (Genesis 12:1-2)

In every time and place some people have believed in one God, while others have believed in many gods, or in none. Some believe that, after they die, they will be reincarnated as another person, or even as an animal; some believe that their soul will survive, while others do not believe in any life beyond the grave. There has been progress in technology and natural science, and customs and structures of society have changed, some for better, some for worse. But knowledge of ultimate meaning concerning God and man, life and death, and the nature of true happiness seems to many as obscure as ever. The deepest thinkers may find answers to such questions on their own, but only after great effort and even the greatest thinkers can still make mistakes.

If we are to find true happiness, God will have to provide in some better way than just leaving us to our own devices. This is the context for the claim that God has indeed provided for human beings by revealing to us what we most need to know. For if the very *existence* of the universe is somehow bound up with the meaning of *human* existence (of rational life), and so with the life of each one of us, then the Creator of the universe, the source of all things, could also be acting within human history to illuminate its meaning. This cannot be dismissed as impossible, but neither can it be determined in advance. It is necessary to actually *look* at human history and judge what claims there are that God has 'spoken'. It is true that there are many religions and more than one great world religion, but neither is there a 'view from nowhere' from which we can comfortably sit and judge everything. We need to start from *somewhere* and be open to the real possibility that God has indeed spoken.

Christian (also Jewish and Muslim) belief is rooted in the claim that God has spoken to the people of Israel. God did not just send out messages to human beings as isolated individuals, but rather chose and formed a particular people. God's revelations were accepted within a *tradition* and a context, a *sacred history* formed by God. When God chose the prophets their whole life was shaped to prepare them for the word they had to speak. Though God has sometimes spoken through an angel or vision, God's word has mostly come by the prophets who were inspired to speak what was in their hearts. The Lord strengthened and guided their words so they would not be mere human words but would really be the voice of God.

These words, of the Law and of the prophets, together with other sacred writings, make up the Holy Scriptures of the Jewish people. In these writings, and through this history, it is possible to hear the word of God.

The twelve tribes of Israel trace their ancestry to Abraham, whom God called from his home in Ur of the Chaldees (modern Iraq) and brought to the Promised Land (*Gn* 12). The story of Abraham is a story of faith. Abraham believed, even when God tested him by asking for the sacrifice of his only son, Isaac. Abraham obeyed, but God provided instead a ram for the sacrifice (*Gn* 22). Isaac lived to a great age and had two sons, Esau and Jacob (later named Israel), who himself had twelve sons after whom the tribes are named (*Gn* 35).

The people of Israel then became slaves in Egypt, but God chose Moses to lead them from Egypt, through the Red Sea and into the desert. This great liberation from slavery is central to the story of the people. It is called the Exodus and is commemorated every year at the feast of the Passover (*Ex* 1-15). In the desert, on Mount Sinai, God gave Moses a Law for the people, the centre of which was the Ten Commandments written on two tablets of stone (*Ex* 19-20, 34). The tablets were kept in a chest called the Ark of the Covenant. The Israelites wandered in the desert for forty years. Then Moses died and Joshua led the people back to the Promised Land (*Dt* 34).

There the people asked for a king (*1 S* 8), and God gave them David, who captured Jerusalem and brought the Ark there (*1 S* 16; *2 S* 5-6). David united the people into a great nation; his son, Solomon, renowned for his wisdom, built a temple for the Ark (*1 K* 4-6). Throughout the history of Israel the people often failed to live according to the Law, and so God inspired prophets to call them to repentance. These prophets, especially Jeremiah, foretold the destruction of Jerusalem its temple on account of the people's wickedness. After this had happened, during the Babylonian exile, the prophets spoke words of comfort, promised a return to Israel, a time of renewal and the coming of a saviour (*Is* 11, 40, 52-53).

Jesus

Jesus, knowing that the Father had given all things into his hands, and that he had come from God and was going to God, rose from supper, laid aside his garments, and girded himself with a towel. Then he poured water into a basin, and began to wash the disciples' feet, and to wipe them with the towel with which he was girded. (John 13:3-5)

The focus of the Catholic religion is not a holy book, but rather a person: Jesus of Nazareth, the saviour promised by the prophets. Jesus is himself the fullness of the revelation given by God. He is the word God has spoken to us. As the Scriptures say, "In many and various ways God spoke to our fathers of old by the prophets; but in these last days he has spoken to us by a Son" (*Heb* 1:1-2). "And the Word became flesh and dwelt among us, full of grace and truth; we have beheld his glory, glory as of the only Son from the Father" (*Jn* 1:14). Jesus came not only to tell us things but chiefly to share with us the very life of God and bring us into a new relationship as children of the Father.

The Father is God. The Son is God: God from God, of one being with the Father. The Son was always with the Father in eternity, but also came to live a human life, in time, taking flesh from his mother, Mary. He was truly and completely human, able to suffer and rejoice, weep and laugh. He was no invulnerable superman, but like us in all things except sin. He did not cease to be God, nor was he just pretending to be human. Jesus is the Divine Word who has taken human form. He is one person in two natures (two ways of existing): always in eternity with his Father, now also in time for our sake. This mystery of God become human is called the Incarnation. When Jesus was raised from the dead he did not *stop* being human. Rather his *human* life was transfigured. He now lives the glorified life we hope to have when we, too, are raised from the dead. Jesus is the bridge between God and human beings. He lived a human life that we might share the Divine life.

Jesus was born of a virgin, Mary, in the village of Bethlehem (near Jerusalem), the son, so it was thought, of Joseph. He was brought up in the northern village of Nazareth in Galilee and lived there as an ordinary working man until he was thirty years old (*Mt* 1-2; *Lk* 1-2). Meanwhile, there was a man known as John the Baptist, a prophet who told the people to repent of their sins and be baptised. Jesus chose to be baptised by John to begin his public ministry. This was not because he had any sins of which to repent, but to show that he would suffer as a sinner to atone for the people (*Mt* 3).

Jesus gathered disciples and chose twelve of them as 'Apostles', the first of whom he called Peter, which means rock (*Mk* 3:13-19). He preached that 'the kingdom of God' was very near and that God's Spirit would soon come down upon the people. He preached the forgiveness of sins and freed corrupt officials ('tax collectors') and prostitutes from their sins (*Lk* 7:37-50, 19:1-10). He was a miracle worker who healed the blind, the lame, and lepers. He fed five thousand people with five loaves and two fishes (*Mt* 14:13-21). He turned water into wine, walked on water and even raised the dead (*Jn* 2:1-11, 6:16-22, 11:1-44). He cast out demons and restored to perfect health those tormented by them (*Mk* 1:21-27, 3:11-12, 5:1-20).

Jesus gained such a great following that the religious and secular leaders began to see him as a threat. One of his Apostles, Judas, betrayed him. After his arrest, Jesus was condemned to death, mocked, flogged and finally crucified for claiming to be "the King of the Jews" (*Jn*

18-19). Jesus had predicted his terrible death, but still he remained faithful to his mission: healing, forgiving and preaching fearlessly right to the very end. Three days after the crucifixion his tomb was found empty, and several times Jesus appeared to his disciples (*Mt* 28, *Mk* 16, *Lk* 24, *Jn* 20-21, *1 Co* 15:3-9). He had risen from the dead! He was taken up into heaven, and from there he sent the Holy Spirit to the waiting disciples (*Ac* 1-2).

Those who believed in him saw Jesus as the Christ, the saviour of the human race promised by the prophets. He had come to save us from the evil we do (sin) and the evil we suffer (sickness and death). The Father raised Jesus from the dead and accepted his whole life as an offering for sinners.

The Forgiveness of Sins

And behold, a woman of the city, who was a sinner, when she learned that Jesus was at table in the Pharisee's house, brought an alabaster flask of ointment. And standing behind him at his feet, weeping, she began to wet his feet with her tears, and wipe them with the hair of her head, and kissed his feet and anointed them with the ointment. (Luke 7:37-38)

The message of the Gospel assumes that there is something deeply wrong with the world, an extreme problem requiring an extreme remedy. When Jesus came among us he healed the sick, reconciled sinners and preached good news. In exchange for this he was betrayed, tortured and executed. He was rejected by his own people, by the Jewish leaders and by the Roman governor. Jesus's death shows in a vivid manner the evil of which human beings are capable. The Scriptures trace the origin of this evil to the first human beings, Adam and Eve, their rejection of God and their subsequent fall from primitive innocence (*Gn* 3). This story becomes more significant in light of the rejection of Jesus. Human beings have repeatedly rejected God, and have even killed his beloved Son. This reveals how low human nature has sunk.

But if God is good, and all things were made good in the beginning, where has all this evil come from? Some people have imagined two gods, good and evil, locked in a fierce struggle for sovereignty. Yet the notion of 'pure evil' makes no sense. Evil is always a defect or deprivation, a sign of something missing, a rip in the fabric of things. Something may exist with defects, but no defect exists on its own. A defect is only the lack of some due perfection. Even the Devil is only a once-powerful angel who has gone off the rails and now wants to spoil it for everyone else. Evil is not a dark force, or a power, or a substance: it is rather the absence of some perfection that ought to be - but is not.

Human malice is, nevertheless, a disturbing reality. It is harmful and seemingly wholly unnecessary. Further, it seems that its manifestations - greed, lust and hypocrisy -

are rooted deeply in the very structures of society. This is evident not only from the death of Jesus, but also from the repeated miseries of human history. We inherit bad blood, as it were, from our parents, an alienation from God that Catholics call 'original sin'. All this is due to the misuse of freedom, by the Devil and the fallen angels, by Adam and Eve, and indeed by all men and women. We are the authors of our own sins and bear responsibility for them and for the harm they do.

Our sins cut us off from God and from each other, for the injustice of sin destroys all relationships, our relationship with God and our relationships with our fellow human beings.

God did not leave us in the mess we made but came to undo the damage and to save his creatures from the harm they had caused. To do this God took on a human nature, living out a full human life so as to atone, by this one innocent life, for all the sins which human beings had, and would, commit. Jesus established a new beginning, based on an honest acknowledgement of sin and an acceptance of Jesus as the saviour. He overcame death, which is the consequence of sin, and after his resurrection he gave the Holy Spirit for the forgiveness of sins. Catholics receive this forgiveness certainly and visibly through the sacraments, but it may be present whenever anyone turns from sin and seeks God's help. It is not that we first turn to God and then God forgives us, but even our turning to

God is due to the spirit of new life and repentance that God inspires in us. God is at work within us drawing us to repent.

Mercy is therefore a fundamental principle of the Christian life. Every Christian relies on mercy and therefore none can afford to neglect showing mercy. It is also necessary to work for a better and a more just society, for the protection of the weak and for honesty in public life. Yet no matter how hard we try, no society will be perfect. We must continue to show mercy to those who have done wrong. This will not mean that we should dispense with rules and laws and punishments, for these offer protection for the vulnerable; but however we safeguard society we must never, in so doing, exclude anyone from mercy. Jesus warned, "Judge not lest you be judged" (*Mt* 7:1), but he promised mercy to the merciful.

The Holy Spirit

Suddenly a sound came from heaven like the rush of a mighty wind, and it filled all the house where they were sitting. And there appeared to them tongues as of fire, distributed and resting on each one of them. And they were all filled with the Holy Spirit and began to speak in other tongues, as the Spirit gave them utterance. (Acts 2:2-4)

Before Jesus died he promised that he would send his followers "another comforter" who was "the Spirit of Truth" (*Jn* 14:25-26, 16:4-15). This was the Holy Spirit whose coming had been predicted by the prophets. On the feast of Pentecost, fifty days after Jesus was crucified, the Holy Spirit came upon Jesus's followers and gave them new confidence (*Ac* 2). The Spirit gave them power to do many miracles and the courage to face martyrdom.

The Holy Spirit is God who comes to us as a gift and gives us a *spiritual* life. Catholics call this gift of God 'sanctifying grace': the gift that makes us holy. By his life and death as one of us, Jesus won for us God's friendship, a share in God's own life. It is Jesus who gives us the Holy Spirit so that we can be united to God as children of the Father, brothers and sisters in Christ. The Spirit changes us from the inside, gives us a new heart and inspires us to live a different kind of life.

The Life of the Spirit is a life of true freedom: not a lawless and destructive freedom, but one grounded on the law of love and the rule of mercy. It causes us to break out of the disorder of our present lives and live according to a true and just order that may seem eccentric in the world's eyes. The gifts of this new Life make us poor in spirit, pure of heart, merciful, peacemakers, hungry and thirsty for justice (*Mt* 5:3-10). Poverty of spirit means being free from the burden of slavery to money, power, status and possessions so we can more easily serve those in need.

These gifts provide the freedom to truly love, for love is the heart of the Gospel and the first effect in us of the Holy Spirit. "God is love, and he who abides in love abides in God, and God abides in him." (*1 Jn* 4:16).

We do not deserve to receive grace (the gift of the Holy Spirit), but it is always the free gift of God. However, once we have received grace God really changes us so we really do deserve heaven. Grace is free but it is not irresistible and we must, co-operate with it. St Augustine once said, "God created us without us, but he will not save us without us". We must freely respond to the free gift of grace. Yet because God is our creator, as well as our redeemer, then God in fact is sustaining all our actions. We cannot even respond to God without God's help. Nevertheless, God has given us a genuine freedom, and when we are given grace we actually become freer and more truly ourselves. The good things we do inspired by grace are not done partly by us and partly by God; rather they are truly our actions and they are *completely dependent* upon grace.

The Holy Spirit is not some impersonal force or power but is God within us. The Holy Spirit is the comforter, a person distinct from the Father and distinct from the Son. Does this mean that there are three gods? No! - for it is not just that there happens to be only one God, as though God were the only member of a class (like the last dodo). All *unity* comes from God. God is one and *must* be one. He is *essentially one*, wholly and complete.

Father, Son, and Spirit are one entity (one God), but there are different someones (different persons). The persons are distinguished not because they are different entities but by their relationships with one another. The Father is Father of the Son. The Son is Son of the Father. The Spirit is Spirit of the Father and the Son. This mystery of the three persons who are one God is called the doctrine of the Holy Trinity.

II. The Body of Christ

The Catholic Church

After this I looked, and behold, a great multitude which no man could number, from every nation, from all tribes and peoples and tongues, standing before the throne and before the Lamb, clothed in white robes, with palm branches in their hands. (Revelation 7:9)

'Church' means 'those gathered together'. Jesus gathered together a group of disciples. He called them, taught them, and then sent them out to preach in his name. In his lifetime he went only to his own people, "the lost sheep of the house of Israel" (*Mt* 15:24), but by his death he fulfilled the new covenant which was to include all the nations in a new people (*1 P* 2:10).

When Jesus was crucified most of his disciples fled (except for Mary, his mother, John his disciple and some of the other women); but after his resurrection Jesus gathered his disciples again and then sent the Holy Spirit upon them at Pentecost. This was the birth of the Church. The earliest Christians attempted to live in a way that was faithful to the teaching of the Apostles, sharing all their possessions so that no one would be in need. They met to pray and celebrate the Eucharist. The Church spread rapidly and welcomed gentile converts as well as Jews. They believed in Jesus and were baptised in his name (*Ac* 2:41-47). The Church is not only a collection of individuals but is a single people gathered into one body, the body of Christ, and living by a common spirit, the Holy Spirit.

Jesus gave authority in the Church to St Peter and the other Apostles who preached the faith and ruled the Church. They appointed or approved leaders and ministers of local churches. Bishops (meaning overseers), priests or presbyters (meaning elders) and deacons (meaning servants) carry on the apostolic ministry and exercise authority in the Church. The bishops together make up a 'college' that has responsibility for the Church as a whole. They are the successors to the Apostles. St Peter and St Paul were martyred in Rome, the capital of the ancient world, and the bishop of Rome (also called the Pope) is accounted first among the bishops, being the successor of St Peter, the first of the Apostles.

Since earliest times some people have been impatient with weak and sinful Christians in the Church. Some have tried to set up rival churches just for the pure. However, Jesus taught that, until the last judgement, the Church would always be a mixed body in which saints and sinners, wheat and weeds, grow together (*Mt* 13:24-30). Sometimes, out of mercy, it is necessary for Christians to correct and discipline their fellow believers. But the attempt, however well intentioned, to create a purified church may result in the exclusion of the weak and confused - in short, the very people whom Jesus came to save. To be a Catholic is to maintain unity with the greater Catholic Church, despite the faults of all her members and leaders, and over and above national, local and personal loyalties.

In her history the Church has suffered from many divisions, but two are most significant. Around 1000 AD the Eastern (Greek-speaking) half of the Church split from the Western (Latin-speaking) half. Today Greek and Russian Orthodox Churches are not in full communion with Rome and no longer accept the authority of the Bishop of Rome. Around 1500 AD the Protestant reformers (such as Luther, Calvin and Cranmer) broke away from the Catholic Church and rejected parts of the Church's constant belief and practice. Setting tradition aside, they followed only what they could find in their own reading of the Bible. They rejected the authority of the Pope and traditional attitudes towards Mary and the saints. They also disputed the Catholic understanding of the Eucharist. These continuing divisions are a scandal (a stumbling block) to non-believers and the movement to overcome them and work for a closer unity of faith and practice among all Christians is called *Ecumenism*.

The Church is the body of Christ without whom there is no salvation. She is one reality, visible and invisible. Yet while baptised Catholics in good faith enjoy the fullness of visible unity, the grace of God is not confined to those in full communion. Those preparing for baptism (catechumens) are joined to the Church by their desire. The Orthodox Church accepts the ancient Christian tradition (for the most part) and enjoys a full sacramental life, having bishops in direct and unbroken succession from the Apostles. All the baptised, of whatever denomination, share in Christ's life. They may bear no fault for being outside full communion with the Catholic Church. Even those who have not heard of Jesus may benefit from his passion and death if, moved by the Holy Spirit, they act out of charity. Only God sees the soul and in the end everyone will be judged according to the light he or she has been given (*Rm* 2:15). No one is excluded from the offer of salvation.

The Scriptures

They said to each other, "Did not our hearts burn within us while he talked to us on the road, while he opened to us the Scriptures?" (Luke 24:32)

The Bible (the Holy Scriptures) is the book of the People of God. Jesus did not write a book but he did found a Church, which relies not only on the written word, inspired by God, but also on the understanding and practice of the Gospel that comes through tradition. "The Church does not draw her certainty about all revealed truths from the Holy Scriptures alone. Hence, both Scripture and Tradition must be accepted and honoured with equal feeling of devotion and reverence" (Second Vatican Council). The Church is the best guide for understanding Scripture, for she herself is guided by the Holy Spirit "into the fullness of truth" (*Jn* 16:13).

Catholics accept as Holy Scripture the forty-six books of the people of Israel: the Old Testament. Some of these books (Tobit, Judith, parts of Esther, Wisdom, Sirach, Baruch, parts of Daniel and 1 and 2 Maccabees) are not accepted as Scripture by modern Jews and are not found in Protestant Bibles, though they are sometimes included in an appendix called the 'Apocrypha'. They were written only a short time before Christ (after 200 BC) and some Jews thought them too recent to be sacred. But this was the Bible of the Early Church and of the Jews of Jesus's own day.

Genesis, the first book of Holy Scripture, tells about the creation and fall of human beings, and about the call of Abraham and his descendants. The next four books, Exodus, Leviticus, Numbers and Deuteronomy, tell the story of Moses and the giving of the Law. Jews call these books the *Torah* (the Law); Christians call them the *Pentateuch*.

Twelve books trace the history of the people of Israel from the time of Moses: Joshua, Judges, 1 and 2 Samuel, 1 and 2 Kings, 1 and 2 Chronicles, Ezra, Nehemiah, and 1 and 2 Maccabees. Five others relate particular stories (mainly) within this history: Ruth, Judith, Esther, Tobit and Job.

The Old Testament also includes Psalms, which consists of 150 songs of prayer and worship, and five 'wisdom' books: Proverbs, Ecclesiastes, Song of Songs, Wisdom, and Sirach (also called Ecclesiasticus).

Finally, there are four books by 'major' prophets: Isaiah, Jeremiah (together with Lamentations and Baruch), Ezekiel, and Daniel; and twelve books by 'minor' prophets: Hosea, Joel, Amos, Obadiah, Jonah, Micah, Nahum, Habakkuk, Zephaniah, Haggai, Zechariah, and Malachi.

In addition to the Old Testament, Catholics hold as Scripture twenty-seven books that have come down to us from the Church of the Apostles.

This collection, known as the New Testament, begins with four accounts of the life of Jesus, the Gospels according to Matthew, Mark, and Luke (sometimes called 'synoptic' because they recount largely the same events in the life of Jesus) and the Gospel according to John. There are minor differences in how the four Gospels recount the story of Jesus because each writer (or 'evangelist') relates the same events in his own way. Their different viewpoints give us a deeper knowledge of who Jesus was - a fuller picture than if there had been only one eyewitness account.

An additional eye-witness account, also by Luke, tells of the spread of the Early Church: the Acts of the Apostles. There then follow 21 letters, 13 of which are attributed to St Paul and named according to whom they were sent: Romans, 1 and 2 Corinthians, Galatians, Ephesians, Philippians, Colossians, 1 and 2 Thessalonians, 1 and 2 Timothy, Titus and Philemon. The Letter to the Hebrews is anonymous. The seven remaining letters are named after the Apostles to whom they are attributed: James, 1 and 2 Peter, 1, 2 and 3 John, and Jude.

The last book of the New Testament, called Revelation or the Apocalypse, is a revealed vision of God's judgement at the end of the world. Its use of terrifying imagery to show forth the power of God gave comfort to early Christians who were facing persecution and martyrdom.

The Bible is thus not one book but rather a collection of books, and to understand them we must first understand what sort of writings they are. We must consider what the human author meant to say, and then see how these words, received by faith within the context of the Church, communicate to us the word of God. The Holy Scriptures are not intended as a guide to secular history or natural science, and in these things they speak according to the customs of their time and place. The Scriptures teach us how to go to heaven, not how the heavens go. The purpose of the Holy Scriptures is to show us our true destiny in Jesus. They are not only a source of information about Jesus, but also the means by which Jesus himself comes into our hearts by the power of his Spirit. "Since, therefore, all that the inspired authors, or sacred writers, affirm should be regarded as affirmed by the Holy Spirit, we must acknowledge that the books of Scripture, firmly, faithfully and without error, teach that truth which God, for the sake of our salvation, wished to see confided to the Sacred Scriptures" (Second Vatican Council).

The Sacraments

*"My flesh is real food, and my blood is real drink. He
who eats my flesh and drinks my blood abides in me,
and I in him." (John 6:55-56)*

A sacrament is an effective sign of the presence of Jesus
in the Church: an outward sign of an inward grace. The
first sign of God's grace is Jesus himself, "the image of the
invisible God" (*Col* 1:15), but the Church shares Jesus's
presence through hearing, sight, touch and taste. The
Church has termed seven such signs as 'sacrament'.

The greatest of all sacraments is the Mass, also called
the *Eucharist*. On the night before he died Jesus celebrated
a Passover meal with his disciples. He took bread and said,
"Take this, all of you, and eat of it, for this is my body
which will be given up for you". After supper he took the
cup, saying, "Take this, all of you, and drink from it, for
this is the chalice of my blood, the blood of the new and
eternal covenant which will be poured out for you and for
many for the forgiveness of sins. Do this in memory of
me." (Eucharistic Prayer I; *Mt* 26:26-29; *Mk* 14:22-25; *Lk*
22:17-20; *1 Co* 11:23-29). In this way Jesus showed his
disciples that his death on the cross would be a sacrifice to
bring forgiveness of sins. Catholics share in that sacrifice
by celebrating Mass (*1 Co* 10:16-18). When a priest or a
bishop says the words of consecration, the bread and wine
really become the body and blood of Jesus. They still retain

the appearances of bread and wine but what they are has changed. This unique and wholly mysterious change the Church calls transubstantiation. In sharing the Eucharist, Catholics share in an effective sign of their unity in love. The Eucharist is essentially a communion and is therefore also called Holy Communion.

There are two sacraments of initiation to the Christian life: Baptism and Confirmation. *Baptism* is the door to all the other sacraments, a new birth that washes away sin and gives the newly baptised person a share in God's own life, which is the Holy Spirit. A priest or deacon is the ordinary minister of Baptism, but anyone can baptise in an emergency. The minister pours water three times on the head of the one being baptised, or immerses him or her in water, pronounces the person's name (often a new 'Christian' name), and says: "I baptise you in the name of the Father, and of the Son, and of the Holy Spirit" (*Mt* 28:19). *Confirmation* is the completion of Baptism by which the bishop (or priest designated by him) consecrates the baptised person as a mature Christian witness and sends the person forth strengthened by the gifts of the Spirit (*Is* 11:2). The bishop anoints with oil the one being confirmed as a sign of the coming of the Holy Spirit (*Is* 61:1).

There are two sacraments of restoration: Confession and Anointing. *Confession*, also called Penance or Reconciliation, is the sacrament by which sins committed after Baptism are forgiven. Although Baptism forgives all sins, an attraction to sin, 'concupiscence', still remains. This sacrament requires that the person has true sorrow for his or her sins, confesses them to a priest - representing Christ himself (*Jn* 20:22-23) - and performs some token action or 'penance' to express their sorrow. Any sin can be forgiven so long as there is genuine sorrow and a willingness to change and make restitution where this is possible. *Anointing of the sick* is the sacrament which gives strength to those who are ill and in danger of death. If God so wishes, this sacrament may bring physical healing or protection (*Mk* 6:13), or it may give courage to endure the illness. The sacrament is intended to 'raise up' the sick person (*Jm* 5:14-16), either in this life or the next. It also grants forgiveness of sins.

There are two sacraments of vocation: Holy Matrimony, or marriage, and Holy Orders. *Marriage* is practised and valued by many people, but among the baptised it is also a sacrament, a sign of the communion in love between Jesus and the Church (*Ep* 5:21-33). In marriage the couple vow to belong to one another exclusively until death, and to be open to the gift of children. A consummated sacramental marriage cannot be dissolved by any human authority (*Mk* 10:1-12). A Catholic may seek a civil divorce, for grave reason, but is not free to remarry unless it can be shown that, for some reason, the first marriage was not valid. (A declaration that an apparent marriage was not in fact valid is called an annulment.) The grace of the sacrament of marriage helps the couple find salvation through marriage, and the ministers of the sacrament are the couple themselves: the priest is only a witness. However, the Church does require all Catholics to be married before a Catholic priest or deacon, or at least with permission for any exception. If Catholics attempt marriage improperly and without permission they are not married at all.

Holy Orders is the sacrament whereby ministers are chosen from the people and set apart to be successors to the Apostles as bishops, priests and deacons. They have responsibility for preaching the Gospel, administering the sacraments and governing the Church. Only a valid bishop with authority derived from the Apostles has the power to ordain a priest. The grace of this sacrament is to make the candidate a worthy servant of the Church who can find his salvation through serving others in this way. All the sacraments relate in some way to the Mass, which is the sign and source of the whole Christian life.

Mary, the Saints and the Angels

When Jesus saw his mother and the disciple whom he loved standing near, he said to his mother, "Woman, behold your son!" Then he said to the disciple, "Behold, your mother!" And from that hour the disciple took her to his own home. (John 19:26-27)

Jesus had no human father. He was born of a virgin. "Behold a virgin shall conceive and bear a son" (*Mt* 1:23; *Is* 7:14). Mary was no ordinary woman but was graced with a special dignity to become the mother of the saviour. When the angel told her what was to happen, she believed and accepted it with her whole heart. She was not only the physical mother of Jesus, but also the handmaid of the Lord and the first disciple of Jesus (*Lk* 1:26-56). It was she who elicited Jesus's first public miracle (*Jn* 2:1-12) and who stood at the foot of the cross when he died (*Jn* 19:25-27). She remained with the other disciples praying and waiting for the Spirit to come at Pentecost (*Ac* 1:14), though she herself had already been overshadowed by the Holy Spirit in a unique way (Lk 1:35).

From the second century AD, Catholics have called Mary 'the New Eve' because of her unique role in salvation history. In accordance with the promise of Genesis 3:15, Mary's faith and fidelity helped reverse the damage caused by Eve's disobedience. She is called 'Ark of the Covenant' because the glory of the Most High overshadowed her and because she carried the word of God inside her, in her womb. She is called the Blessed Virgin Mary because Catholics have always believed that she remained a virgin - before, during and after the birth of Jesus - and that she had no other children. James and Joseph and others whom the Gospels call 'brothers' of Jesus (a broader term in the language of the time than in modern English) were close relations of Jesus but not, in fact, children of Mary. They may have been his first cousins (perhaps son of her sister, Mary of Clopas - Jn 19:25; Mt 27:56).

Jesus is God among us, the Saviour of the human race, the Redeemer. Mary is in no way equal to Jesus, but she is the one who co-operated most intimately in the work of salvation and received most abundantly of his grace. She is the most perfectly redeemed person, more holy than any other saint could be. She was saved from sin, not by falling and then repenting, but by being preserved always in God's grace, even before her birth, so that she would be worthy to fulfil her role as 'mother of God'. This belief is called the Immaculate Conception. At the end of her life, the Lord did not allow her to see the corruption of the tomb since from her own body she marvellously brought forth that God's incarnate Son, the Author of all Life (*Roman Missal*, Preface of the Assumption). She was taken body and soul into heaven to be with her Son, fulfilling the prophecy, "Go up Lord to the place of your rest, you and the Ark of your Strength" (*Ps* 132:8; see *Rv* 11:19-12:17). This doctrine is called the Assumption.

Mary, whom Catholics also refer to as 'Our Lady', should always be seen in relation to her Son - never on her own. But Jesus should also be seen in relation to Mary, as well as in relation to his disciples and friends. We then see Jesus as a real human being and we see his effect on the lives of others. In much the same way, the Church throughout history has pointed to the saints - those holy, wise and heroic people who have followed Jesus most closely: Perpetua and Felicity, George and Athanasius, Augustine and Aquinas, Francis and Dominic, Thérèse of Lisieux and Edith Stein - all these and other saints show us something more about Jesus himself.

Like the saints, the angels also serve God. Unlike the saints, the angels are pure spirits who have no natural kinship with us. They have become our friends because their life is to do the will of God, and God has great love for his human creatures. Jesus taught us that every little one (that is, every human being) has an angel whose job it is to watch over and pray for us (*Mt* 18:10). This is our 'guardian angel'.

Jesus told us to pray for one another. The saints and the angels constantly pray for us (*Rv* 8:4), intercede on our behalf, and rejoice when we ask for their prayers. Christians can always pray directly to God (there is no obstacle to this, after all, we are his children), but we should also welcome the friendship of the saints and angels and ask for their help. For, the prayer of the righteous person has great power (*Jm* 5:16-19). It is good to have favourite saints, like special friends - to learn about them, follow their example and seek their special intercession. But Catholics believe that among the saints Mary, as queen of the saints and angels, and mother of all Christians, is their greatest friend, example and intercessor. And now that she can never be separated from her Son, she continues in heaven to care for her many children (*Rv* 12:17). The most common prayer addressed to her is the 'Hail Mary':

Hail Mary, full of grace, the Lord is with thee,
Blessed art thou amongst women,
And blessed is the fruit of thy womb, Jesus.
Holy Mary, Mother of God,
Pray for us sinners
Now and at the hour of our death. Amen.

(cf. *Lk* 1:28, 42)

III. The Spiritual Life

Faith

"And I tell you, you are Peter, and on this rock I will build my Church, and the powers of death shall not prevail against it. I will give you the keys of the kingdom of heaven, and whatever you bind on earth shall be bound in heaven, and whatever you loose on earth shall be loosed in heaven." (Matthew 16:18-19)

Faith, which is inseparable from holiness, is a disposition to trust God. But it is not something we can learn with effort and hard work. Rather, it is a gift from God. We cannot save ourselves, and the more proud and self-confident we are, the further we are from the only source of salvation. Faith therefore must begin with the humility to recognise that we need help, not just from other people, but most especially from God. It is not demeaning to rely on God's help; it only reflects our real situation. We can only find fulfilment by accepting God's gracious help: "You made us for yourself and our hearts are restless till they rest in you" (St Augustine).

Abraham provides the great example of faith in the Old Testament. Although he had never heard of Jesus, he put his faith in God's promises and God blessed him richly for his belief. Mary is the great example of faith in the New Testament. She believed the word spoken to her by an angel and rejoiced in accepting Christ as her son.

Faith, then, is fundamentally an adherence of the whole person. For someone who has accepted that God is revealed to us in Jesus, faith involves an assent of the intellect and will to the self-revelation God has made through Jesus's deeds and words. Much of this self-revelation is very clearly stated in the New Testament. By faith Christians believe that Jesus died for our sake and that he rose from the dead on the third day. Yet throughout history there have been fierce disputes among Christians about how to understand who Jesus is, and what he has done for us. To resolve such disputes the bishops of the Church have gathered together to clarify the Gospel they have received. Some of these gatherings, which have been ratified by the Pope, the successor of St Peter, authoritatively represent the view of the Church as a whole. These are called 'ecumenical councils'. The solemn declarations of an ecumenical council, and the most solemn statements a Pope can make, are guarded by the Holy Spirit against error. They are infallible and all Catholics are bound to believe them as truths of the Catholic faith.

The First Ecumenical Council was held at Nicea in 325 AD and gave us the profession of faith that we call the Nicene Creed (the word 'creed' comes from the Latin 'credo', which means 'I believe'). In the first thousand years of the Church there were eight ecumenical councils, all held in the Eastern part of the Church: Nicea, Constantinople, Ephesus, Chalcedon, Constantinople II, III, Nicea II, and Constantinople IV. These were mainly about how Jesus could be both truly God and truly man at the same time.

There were ten ecumenical councils in the middle ages, all held in the Western part of the Church: Lateran I-IV, Lyons I, II, Vienne, Constance, Florence, Lateran V. These were mainly about the Church and the sacraments.

The Council of Trent, which was held in the sixteenth century, defended the Catholic understanding of the sacraments. Three centuries later in 1870, Vatican I stated that the Pope could speak infallibly, on faith and morals, even outside an ecumenical council. The most recent council, Vatican II (1963-1965), presented Catholicism in a modern way, encouraged ecumenism and commissioned the renewal of the Liturgy. It was after Vatican II that the Church began sometimes to celebrate Mass in English and in other modern languages. In the Western part of the Church from the third century until 1965 the Mass was celebrated only in Latin.

The Church still uses the ancient Apostles' Creed which predates the first ecumenical council. It reads as follows:

I believe in God, the Father almighty, Creator of heaven and earth.

And in Jesus Christ, his only Son, our Lord, who was conceived from the Holy Spirit, born of the Virgin Mary, suffered under Pontius Pilate, was crucified, died, and was buried; he descended into hell; on the third day he rose again from the dead; he ascended into heaven, and is seated at the right hand of God the Father Almighty; from there he will come to judge the living and the dead.

I believe in the Holy Spirit, the holy catholic Church, the communion of saints, the forgiveness of sins, the resurrection of the body, and life everlasting. Amen.

Prayer

In the days of his flesh, Jesus offered up prayers and supplications, with loud cries and tears, to him who was able to save him from death, and he was heard for his godly fear. (Hebrews 5:7)

Faith that God will provide for all our needs gives rise to hope, and the first expression of this hope is to pray that these needs will be met. Jesus often told his disciples to pray for whatever they needed: "Ask and it will be given you, seek and you will find" (*Mt* 7:7). Sometimes God gives us what we ask for; sometimes, for reasons we do not fully understand, God chooses to give us something else instead. However, no sincere prayer goes unheard and God always provides for our deepest needs. Jesus taught us how to pray in these words (*Mt* 6:9-13):

Our Father, who art in heaven,
Hallowed by thy name.
Thy Kingdom come.
Thy will be done on earth, as it is in heaven.
Give us this day our daily bread,
And forgive us our trespasses,
As we forgive those who trespass against us,
And lead us not into temptation,
But deliver us from evil. Amen.

As well as praying for themselves and for others, Christians also give thanks to God, praise him and meditate on what he has done. All these activities are called prayer, which, in this wider sense, is the raising of heart and mind to God. All Christian prayers are a way of sharing in Jesus's prayer to the Father. Jesus offered his whole life to his Father and made his death into an offering. This most important public prayer (or 'Liturgy') is the Sacrifice of the Mass, which is a true participation in the offering of Jesus on the cross. All Catholics are bound to attend Mass and rest from unnecessary work on Sunday, the day of the Resurrection.

From ancient times the Church has developed a regular pattern of daily prayer called the Divine Office: Office of Readings (Matins), Morning Prayer (Lauds), Prayer during the Day (Terce, Sext, None), Evening Prayer (Vespers), and Night Prayer (Compline). Each consists of

Psalms and scriptural songs, readings and other prayers. All priests are obliged to pray the Office and it is sung publicly in many religious houses. Many lay people find Morning and Evening Prayer helpful. Apart from the daily cycle of prayers, there is also a pattern for the week, and liturgical seasons throughout the year.

The main feasts of the liturgical year are the birth of Jesus (Christmas), preceded by four weeks of Advent, and the commemoration of his death and resurrection (Easter), preceded by six weeks of Lent. Easter is the year's most important feast. The main services are on Holy Thursday evening, Good Friday afternoon and the Easter Vigil on Holy Saturday night. Catholics traditionally do some penance during Lent, usually giving up some luxury or performing some good work.

The Epiphany (6 January) recalls the wise men who visited the Christ Child. The Ascension, which occurs forty days after Easter (on a Thursday), commemorates Jesus's ascending into heaven. In England and Wales and some other countries, the Epiphany and Ascension are celebrated on the Sunday closest to the day. Pentecost Sunday, ten days after the Ascension, celebrates the coming of the Holy Spirit. After Pentecost comes Trinity Sunday, and the Thursday after that is the feast of Corpus Christi (celebrating the presence of the body of Christ in the Eucharist), in England and Wales this feast has also been moved to the nearest Sunday. Additional feast days throughout the year include those dedicated to the saints. Of these, the Assumption (15 August) is so important that on that day Catholics everywhere are obliged to attend Mass. Ash Wednesday (the first day of Lent) and the commemoration of All Souls (2 November) are not obligatory but they are popular days to attend Mass.

One of the most popular Catholic forms of private prayer and devotion is the Rosary, which consists in reciting 'Our Father's and 'Hail Mary's while meditating on some events in the lives of Jesus and Mary. There are twenty such events or 'mysteries': five of joy, five of light, five of sorrow, five of glory. Catholics also make use of statues, images and crucifixes to help focus their mind while praying to Jesus, Mary or the saints. Sometimes Catholics will visit the tomb of a saint, or take some article touched by them, or even a tiny bone belonging to them, as a memento or 'relic', just as in the Scriptures people took handkerchiefs that had touched St Paul and carried them to the sick, who were then miraculously healed (*Ac* 19:12). Thus relics, crucifixes, statues, physical gestures (like making the sign of the cross, which Christians have done since the second century) are useful for us, as Jesus showed. For God came to us in Christ in a physical way. The Word became flesh, not just thoughts or mere words.

Charity

*God is love and he who abides in love abides in God,
and God abides in him. (1 John 4:16)*

Of all the virtues that make someone holy the most
important is love. Jesus taught that love was the meaning
and point of God's law. He said that the two most important
commandments of the law were "You shall love the Lord
your God with all your heart, and with all your soul, and
with all you mind" and "You shall love your neighbour as
yourself" (*Mt* 22:36-39). Before he died, Jesus gave the
disciples a commandment of his own, "Love one another
as I have loved you" (*Jn* 13:34). When Jesus was asked
about the commandment to love one's neighbour he told
this parable:

> A man on his way to Jericho was robbed and beaten
> and left half dead. A Priest and a Levite came by, but
> they ignored the man. Finally a Samaritan came by.
> [Jews at this time avoided the Samaritans because they
> regarded them as being unfaithful to the Jewish law.]
> The Samaritan brought the man to an inn and took care
> of him. Which one was the neighbour to that man? The
> one who showed mercy. So go and do likewise.

> (cf. Luke 10:25-37)

Out of a desire to live perfectly in love some men and
women abandon the possibility of family, position

and wealth and devote themselves to a life of prayer in community, sharing all their possessions and submitting their will to a designated superior. Communities of monks, nuns or friars live according to a rule which derives a distinctive character (a *charism*) from the founder. This may be to preach, to teach or to tend the sick, or it may be to live an enclosed life of strict discipline and silence. There are many forms of religious life, founded at different times with different characters, each of which adds something to the life of the Church as a whole.

However, perfect charity (which is love that comes from God) does not require an extra act of public dedication (like that of a monk or nun), but can inspire every sort of Christian life, single or married, lay or religious. Charity is the life and soul of all the other virtues, giving them direction and purpose. If our actions are not done out of love then it does not matter how well they are done; they are not the actions of a holy person. But good actions must also show good sense and fairness. If an action is unjust it cannot be loving; likewise, loving one person can never be an excuse for treating another person unjustly.

As well as possessing prudence and justice it is necessary to be the sort of person who can act well in difficult situations. To be loving in some situations will also require courage, and in other situations it will require moderation and self-restraint. Our appetites for food and drink, for sexual satisfaction, or for any other pleasure need to be measured by the reality of the situation and the human values involved. With food, drink and drugs this primarily means what is reasonable for health. However, we should also sometimes feast, to celebrate; and at other times fast, to gain self-knowledge and help us to pray.

In sexual matters the measure of value is the family, for sexual affection expresses an intimate committed relationship and is ordered towards sustaining married love and having children. With couples who are not married what shows of affection are reasonable depends on the character of the relationship, for some expressions of romantic affection are quite proper in those who are free to marry and are seeking a partner for life. Yet complete sexual union is proper only to marriage, and engaging in sexual relations outside marriage is intrinsically dishonest and is irresponsible in that it risks the well-being of a child who might be the fruit of such love. If a woman conceives in difficult circumstances it is the duty of all involved to support her for her sake and for the sake of the child, for abortion is morally no different from infanticide, however it may be disguised.

Charity is not just a 'private' virtue but should lead to social action. This might mean working for the needy or seeking justice for those who have been unfairly treated. Every society is imperfect and Catholics should seek to help those who suffer most. The virtue of charity is not peculiar to baptised Christians, but is the heart of the Christian message and the measure of genuine Christianity.

Eternal Life

*The dead man came out, his hands and feet bound
with bandages, and his face wrapped with a cloth.
Jesus said to them, "Unbind him, and let him go."
(John 11:44)*

The Gospel, the good news for those who accept Jesus as
their saviour, is the promise of salvation. Salvation means
being saved from sin, suffering and death so as to live a
new and joyful life. This life begins as soon as one becomes
Christian, at Baptism. It begins with the forgiveness of
sins, and with the faith, hope and charity (*1 Co* 13:13) that
make up the Christian life. It is not just 'pie in the sky
when you die' - it begins here and now in this life.

Part of the hope that sustains us in this life is the promise
that death is not the end. Jesus was betrayed, tortured and
killed, but on the third day he rose from the dead. He really
died, but he was raised up from death. He did not simply
return to the kind of mortal life he had lived before (as
Lazarus did); Jesus was transformed and went on to live a
life we cannot understand, a life we call 'glory', which is a
direct share in God's immortality.

Each of us will die and that death will be for us the
moment of truth. Our bodies are buried in the ground or
burned, but something of us, our soul, does not die with
the body. The soul will be judged according to whether we
have loved and shown mercy to others (*Mt* 25:31-46). Yet

no matter how wicked people have been in life they can still receive forgiveness, provided they repent before death catches up with them. It is God's desire that all should be saved and no one is left without the opportunity to find mercy. Only those who stubbornly cling to their sins are finally lost. This ultimate loss of God is called 'hell'.

There is an essential and important difference between mortal sin, which is an act by which we utterly reject God, and venial sin, which is a small failure or lapse, a vice that is neither so serious nor so deliberate as to constitute a rejection of God's life. All Christians commit venial sins, but mortal sins can be avoided. If we fall into mortal sin we must repent before we can regain spiritual life. For those who have turned to God and do repent, but half-heartedly, and with many little faults still clinging to them, there is still hope. By God's grace their faith and love will save them, but only 'as through fire' (*1 Co* 3:15). They must first undergo a season of sorrow for the venial sins they did not fully reject during life. This process of purging in death, by which the imperfectly repentant sinner is made into a perfect saint, is called 'purgatory'. The souls in purgatory may be helped by our prayers and the Church has always encouraged the devout practice of praying for the dead, especially by offering Mass, which is the principal prayer of the Church.

The souls of the dead are rewarded or punished, but this is not the end of the story. My soul is not myself; it is only part of me. If my body is not saved then I am not saved. God came among us, not as an angel, but as a human being, in the flesh. So also Jesus is present to us by material signs in the sacraments of the Church which is his body. When Jesus rose from the dead, he did so in a body, glorified and transformed, but a real body nonetheless. The tomb was empty, for his body was taken up with him in glory. Christian hope, then, is for a resurrection of the body.

Jesus promised that one day he would come again in glory, the whole world would come to an end and all the dead would be raised in their bodies (*Mt* 24; *Jn* 5:28-29). There will be a new heaven and a new earth (*Rv* 21:1). Obviously we do not know what such a glorified world will be like. "No eye has seen, nor ear heard, nor the heart of man conceived, what God has prepared for those who love him" (*1 Co* 2:9). Yet it is important that not only every individual but every collective, every nation and institution, and all history will come under judgement. And in this new world everything good in our transient world will be taken up into God's eternal presence and find its place. All that has been left unresolved in this life will be resolved, every tear will be wiped away, friends will be reunited and there will be no more shadows, no sacraments or religion, for God will be seen by all and will be all in all.

Catholicism

*"I thank thee, Father, Lord of heaven and earth,
that thou hast hidden these things from the wise
and understanding and revealed them to babes."
(Matthew 11:25)*

Catholicism is not an island, it is a continent, a whole
world extending across two thousand years and embracing
more than one billion people in every country on earth. It
completely permeates the roots of Western culture, art and
literature, from the beginnings of modern science in the
thirteenth century, to the foundations of nursing and mass
education in the nineteenth century (to make no mention of
the development of brewing!) It is not just that there have
been Catholics who have contributed to the arts, sciences
and humanities, but, in certain cases at least, they have
brought with them a greater depth and vision precisely
because of their faith. In the music of Palestrina, Elgar
or Messiaen, the poetry of Dante, the painting of Giotto,
Fra Angelico or Michelangelo, the plays of Shakespeare
(which certain express a Catholic vision, though the
pattern of his own religious practice is disputed), the
novels of Evelyn Waugh, Francoise Mauriac, or Flannery
O'Connor (the list could be extended indefinitely), one
can clearly trace a Catholic spirit. One can see this also
in other fields, in the contribution of E.F. Schumacher to
environmental economics, of Mary Douglas and René

Girard to anthropology, of Elizabeth Anscombe and Alasdair MacIntyre to contemporary philosophy. The Catholic spirit exists not just in Europe but on every continent, and every country has its own expression of the faith, from the martyrs of Nagasaki to the apparition of Our Lady of Guadalupe.

The Catholic faith thus touches every aspect of life and excludes none. So what is attractive in the faith, and what the faith inspires someone to do is as infinitely variable as the human spirit. What is essential is to relate the faith to the rest of one's life and see how a faith in the creator and redeemer of every human reality can deepen one's appreciation of what it is to be human. This may not necessarily mean reading Catholic authors (even in the partisan field of Reformation history, one of the most illuminating modern contributions has been made by Oxford historian Christopher Haigh, who is not himself Catholic). But it will mean trying to cultivate a Catholic way of thinking.

What then should someone do if he or she is interested in becoming Catholic? First find a Catholic Church and start going to Mass regularly each Sunday. Try to find some friendly practising Catholics and a sympathetic priest. Get a copy of the Bible, preferably a Catholic translation (such as the Jerusalem or the Catholic edition of the RSV); there is nothing wrong with Protestant translations, but they are missing some books (like Wisdom and Tobit). Buy a copy of the *Simple Prayer Book* (Catholic Truth Society) as it contains the words of the Mass as well as many other useful prayers.

If you are not used to praying, try praying regularly each day. Read one of the Gospels and listen to the readings and homily at Mass. There are many books about the faith and many lives of saints, any of which may be helpful to some people but not to others. The *Catechism of the Catholic Church* is the reference text *par excellence* (but it is hardly bedtime reading!).

As well as going to Church and reading good books it may be necessary to think about what aspects of one's life need changing, and to think of what else one should be doing. Many Catholics are rather passive about their faith, but faith should lead to practice, and many more people could and should be involved in social action: for development overseas; for justice on behalf of the unborn; against the proliferation of weapons of mass destruction and other indiscriminate weapons; for decent treatment of immigrants; for the environment. In short, they could be involved in all kinds of justice, civil rights or peace work.

It is not necessary to come to Church with a clean past, for the Church is for sinners; but it is necessary to examine one's life, be willing to change, and try to put the faith into action. To become a Catholic one only has to approach a priest who might run a regular group, or give individual instruction. The whole process takes many weeks so that no one can be received before he or she has had time to consider things properly and with some informed help. Becoming Catholic is not just some extraordinary event that you might read about in the biography of some famous person (like Oscar Wilde or John Wayne). It is the kind of process that is both wonderful and wonderfully common, both extraordinary and ordinary, like falling in love, or like the birth of a child. It is a journey that many have made but for each one it is something profound and sometimes painful. Taking the step to become a Catholic requires courage as well as faith and perhaps the humility to overcome previous prejudices, but there is no worthwhile goal in life that does not take courage.

Some suggestions for further reading

As Jesus did not write a book, but founded a Church, the best way to find out about the Catholic faith is to make contact with the local Catholic community, and get to know individual practising Catholics, especially priests or religious (monks, nuns, friars, or sisters) who have reflected deeply on the faith. Nevertheless, books can also be useful, especially for people who like to read and to find out things for themselves. Because the Church has existed through two thousand years and in so many places and cultures, there are many great books on the Catholic faith. The selection here is provided as a beginning, an invitation into a world of thought, prayer, and reflection. It is drawn from books that I have found helpful or that I know others have found helpful. Another useful resource is to browse the list of CTS publications, which cover a wide range of topics. With a whole world to discover it is less important where to start than to start somewhere.

Essentials

Simple Prayer book (Catholic Truth Society, 2011) [A very good selection of favourite Catholic prayers and also the words of the Mass, make sure you have an updated copy from 2011 or after, as this will have the new translation of the Mass].

The Bible [the Catholic edition of the RSV is readable and reliable, or you may prefer the Jerusalem Bible which is used for the readings in Church, but the most important thing is to get a Bible with all the books in, or you will be missing out].

Butler's Lives of Saints (Dover Publications, 2005 - or editions by other publishers).

Catechism of the Catholic Church (Continuum, 2000).

Further reading

Chesterton, G.K. *Orthodoxy* (Ignatius Press, 1995 - or editions by other publishers).

Longenecker, D. (ed) *The Path to Rome - Modern Journeys to the Catholic Church* (Gracewing, 2010).

McCabe, H. *God Matters* (Continuum, 1999).

McCabe, H. *The Teaching of the Catholic Church: A New Catechism of Christian Doctrine* (Darton, Longman and Todd, 2000).

O'Collins, G., Venturini M., and Venturini, S.J. *Believing: Understanding the Creed* (Continuum, 1992).

Pinsent, A and M. Holden, *Apologia: Catholic Answers to Today's Questions* (Catholic Truth Society, 2010).

Radcliffe, T. *What is the Point of Being a Christian?* (Continuum, 2005).

Strange, R. *The Catholic Faith* (Darton, Longman and Todd, 1996).

Vann, G. *The Divine Pity: A Study in the Social Implications of the Beatitudes* (Scepter Publishers, 2007 - or editions by other publishers).

Wang, S. *What is the Catholic Church?* (Catholic Truth Society, 2007).

By and about Saints

Autobiography of a Saint (or Story of a Soul) by St Thérèse of Lisieux (many editions).

The Confessions of St Augustine (many editions).

Early Christian Writings (Penguin Classics, 1987).

Introduction to the Devout Life by St Francis de Sales (many editions).

Muggeridge, M. *Something beautiful for God: Mother Teresa of Calcutta* (HarperCollins, 1997 - or editions by other publishers).

For reference (try your local library)

The New Catholic Encyclopaedia (McGraw-Hill, 1967) [The 1913 *Catholic Encyclopaedia* is available online but the 1967 *New Catholic Encyclopaedia* is more readable, reliable and up to date. There have also been several supplements published since the 1967 edition was published].

The Navarre Bible Commentaries (Four Courts, various dates).

The New Jerome Biblical Commentary (Geoffrey Chapman, 1989).

For more information about the Catholic faith:
Please contact your local Catholic parish.